The Bug Hut has a rug.

Bud can sit on that rug.

The Bug Hut has a table.

Do you see that mug up on the table?

The Bug Hut has a mug.

Bud can sip it. Hot!

The Bug Hut has a bed.

Bud can nap on that bed.

Here is Bud the bug.

See Bud go in the Bug Hut.

The Bug Hut has a chair.

Bud has it in the sun.

See Bud sit. Bud has the mug. Bud, you have a fun Bug Hut!

Bud's Bug Hut

Written by Marjorie Curtis
Illustrated by Kathi Ember

Scott Foresman

Phonics Skill: Review

High-Frequency Words: you, that, go

Scott Foresman Reading

Kindergarten Reader 36

Phonics Skill: Review

High-Frequency Words:
you, that, go

Scott Foresman

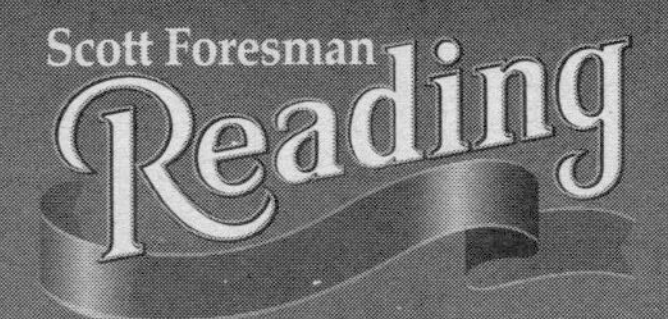

scottforesman.com

Bud's Bug Hut

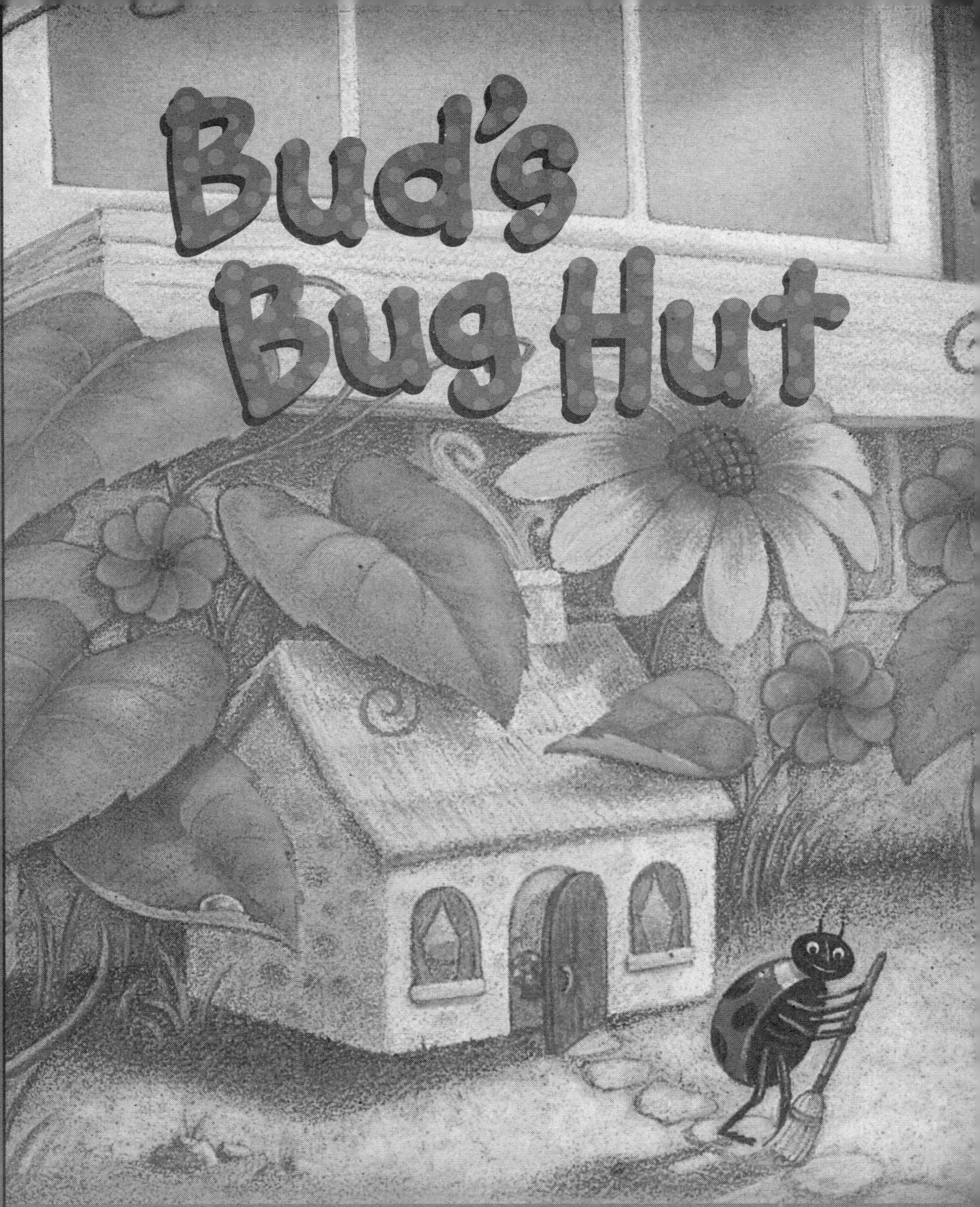

Written by Marjorie Curtis
Illustrated by Kathi Ember

Look at you!

You run up that hill.

Look at you!

One, two, three, go!

Look at you!

You hid up here.

Look at you!

You got on top.

Look at you!

You fit on that rug.

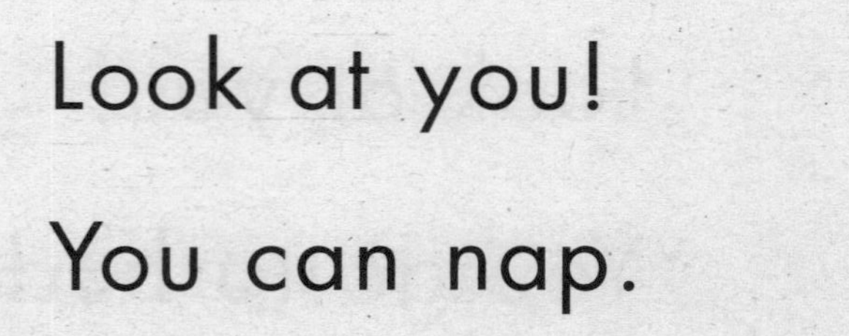

Look at you!

You can nap.

Look at you!

You go to bed.

Look!

Written by K.D. Gill

Scott Foresman

Phonics Skill: Short Vowel Review

High-Frequency Words: you, that, go

Photo Credits
front cover, title page, 2, 3, 4, 8: Ron Kimball. 5, 6, 7:Animals Animals/Robert Maier

Scott Foresman **Reading**

Kindergarten Reader 35

Phonics Skill:
Short Vowel Review

High-Frequency Words:
you, that, go

scottforesman.com

Look!

Written by K.D. Gill

Look what Tom can do!

Mom can lend a hand.

The nest is soft.

It is not damp.

Jen can not swim in the nest.

But Jen can rest in the nest.

Where can Jen get a rest?

Tom and Mom plan a nest.

Jen is a fat round hen.

Mom and Tom like Jen.

Jen can not skip in the nest.

But Jen can nap in the nest.

See what we can do.

One, two, three — clap.

Jen the Hen

Written by Philip Senior
Photographs by John Paul Endress

Scott Foresman

Phonics Skill: Consonant Blends

High-Frequency Words: get, where, and

Scott Foresman Reading

Kindergarten Reader 34

Phonics Skill:
Consonant Blends

High-Frequency Words:
get, where, and

scottforesman.com

Jen the Hen

Written by Philip Senior
Photographs by John Paul Endress

"Where is my pan?

I can fix an egg in my pan."

The pan is yellow and big.

But the pan is not hot.

"I can get the pan hot!

Look at the hot pan!"

We can not fix the egg.

But the man can fix the egg.

We see a big egg.

What can we do?

"Get a fan!

Fan the hot pan!"

We do not like the egg.

The egg is not yellow.

We can fix a ham.

The Man, the Pan, and the Egg

Written by Pamela Gould
Ilustrated by Randy Verougstraete

Scott Foresman

Phonics Skill: Consonant Review

High-Frequency Words: get, where, and

Scott Foresman Reading

Kindergarten Reader 33

Phonics Skill:
Consonant Review

High-Frequency Words:
get, where, and

scottforesman.com

The Man, the Pan, and the Egg

Written by Pamela Gould
Illustrated by Randy Verougstraete

Here is Sam.

Here is Pam.

Here is the bus.

The bus is in the mud.

Look up the hill to the car!

Here is Dan.

Here is Bob.

Here is the car.

The truck is in the mud.

Look up the hill to the bus!

Here is Bud.

Here is the truck.

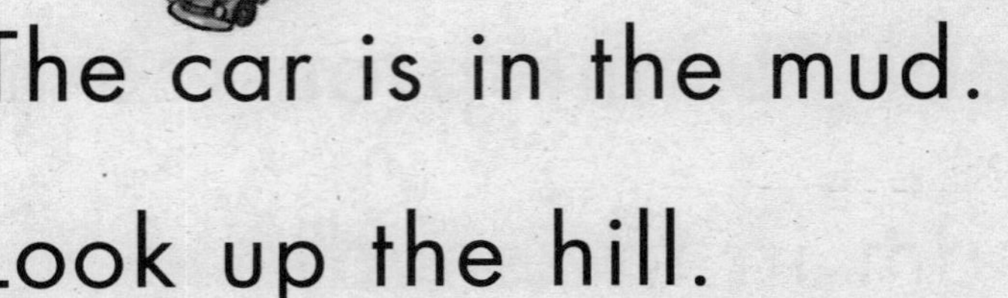

The car is in the mud.

Look up the hill.

Look, I am up on the hill!

I am in the mud!

In the Mud!

Written by Reese Joseph
Illustrated by Abby Cater

Scott Foresman

Phonics Skill: Short Vowel *u*

High-Frequency Words: here, to, up

Scott Foresman Reading

Kindergarten Reader 32

Phonics Skill:
Short Vowel *u*

High-Frequency Words:
here, to, up

scottforesman.com

In the Mud!

Written by Reese Joseph
Illustrated by Abby Cater

Is it a little van?

Is Zebra up in a little van?

It is not a little van.

It is a big yellow van.

Can three get in to the van?

Three can get in to the van.

It is not a yellow jet.

It is a yellow van.

Is it a yellow jet?

Is it a zebra up in a yellow jet?

The yellow van is here.

The van is at the zoo.

We like the yellow van.

We like Zebra and the yellow van.

Zebra and the Yellow Van

Written by Philip Elias
Illustrated by John Steven Gurney

Scott Foresman

Phonics Skill: Consonant *Zz*

High-Frequency Words: here, to, up

Scott Foresman Reading

Kindergarten Reader 31

Phonics Skill:
Consonant Zz

High-Frequency Words:
here, to, up

scottforesman.com

Zebra and the Yellow Van

Written by Philip Elias
Illustrated by John Steven Gurney

I am Pam.

Yes, I have big teeth.

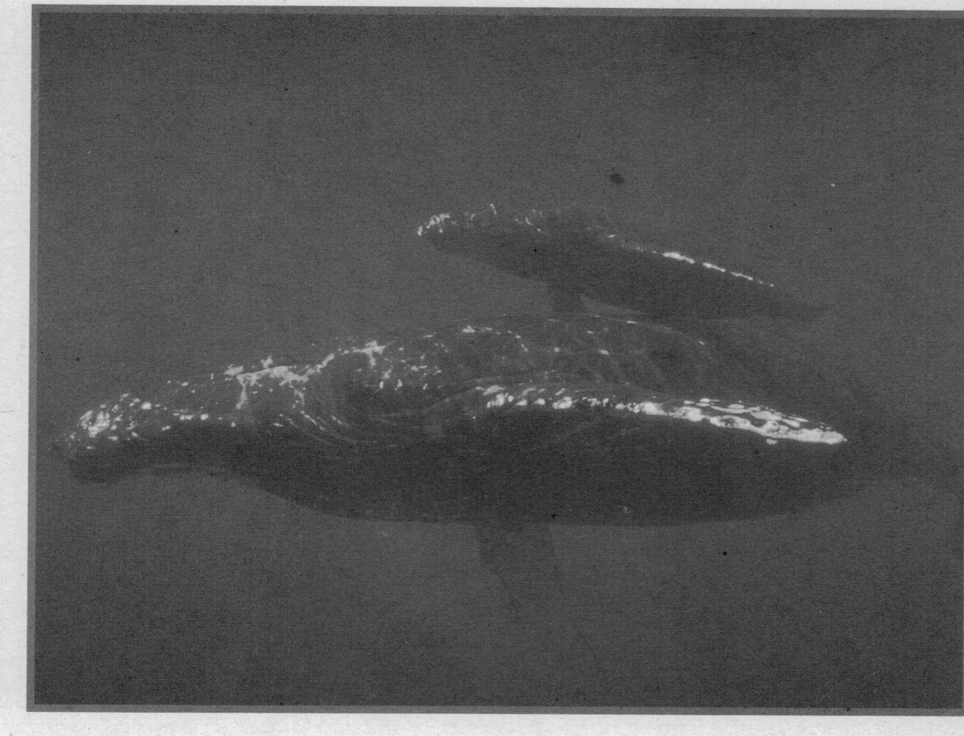

What can we see?

Yes, it is a little whale.

One whale can hop in

the red and yellow sun.

Look at Dot.

Dot is a big blue whale.

I am Ben.

Look at my mom. 

Yes, we like blue water.

Look at what two whales can do!

Blue whale

Beluga whale

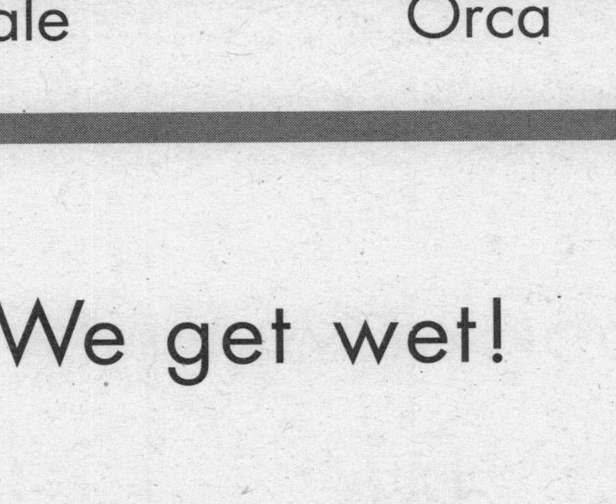

Humpback whale

Orca

Yes! We get wet!

Yes! We Get Wet!

Written by Eileen Kelly

Scott Foresman

Phonics Skill: Consonant *Yy*

High-Frequency Words: red, blue, yellow

Scott Foresman **Reading**

Kindergarten Reader 30

Phonics Skill:
Consonant *Yy*

High-Frequency Words:
red, blue, yellow

scottforesman.com

Yes! We Get Wet!

Written by Eileen Kelly

and a big, yellow hat,

and a big, yellow cat,

and a big, red pen,

sat a big, big fox,

In a big, blue box,

and a big, big hen,

and six little, little chicks.

A Big, Blue Box

Written by Carolyn Rossetti
Illustrated by Patti Boyd

Scott Foresman

This book belongs to

____

Phonics Skill: Consonant *Xx*

High-Frequency Words: red, blue, yellow

Scott Foresman Reading

Kindergarten Reader 29

Phonics Skill:
Consonant Xx

High-Frequency Words:
red, blue, yellow

scottforesman.com

A Big, Blue Box

Written by Carolyn Rossetti
Illustrated by Patti Boyd

Peg Pig got Cat.

Cat, Cat! Jen is in bed!

Jen is red.

Two in bed.

Peg Pig got Bear.

Bear! Bear! Len is in bed.

Ben is red.

One in bed.

Peg Pig got Hen.

Hen, Hen! Ben is in bed!

Len is red.

Three in bed.

One, two, three! Not sick!

Not in bed! Not red!

Sick in Bed?

Written by Lyle Alden
Illustrated by Yuri Salzman

Scott Foresman

Phonics Skill: Short Vowel *e*

High-Frequency Words: one, two, three

Kindergarten Reader 28

Phonics Skill:
Short Vowel *e*

High-Frequency Words:
one, two, three

scottforesman.com

Sick in Bed?

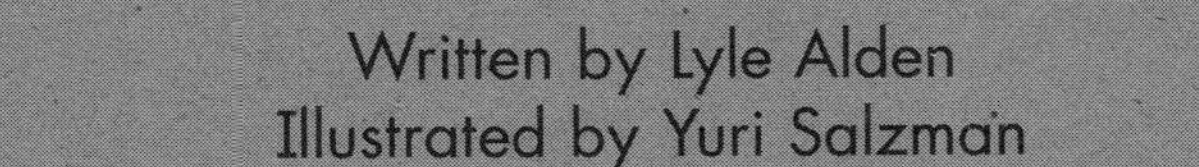

Written by Lyle Alden
Illustrated by Yuri Salzman

What can the duck do?

The duck is bad.

What can the queen do?

The queen is mad.

Bad, bad duck.

Can duck win?

One, two, three.

The queen can see the duck.

One, two, three.

The duck can see the queen.

Mad, mad queen.

Can queen win?

One, two, three.

Two can win.

One, Two, Three

Written by Pat Rashid
Illustrated by Alexi Natchev

Scott Foresman

Phonics Skill: Consonant *Qq*

High-Frequency Words: one, two three

Kindergarten Reader 27

Phonics Skill:
Consonant Qq

High-Frequency Words:
one, two, three

Scott Foresman

scottforesman.com

One, Two, Three

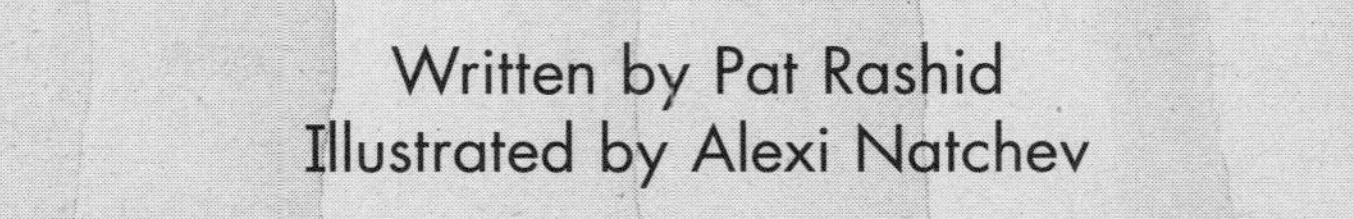

Written by Pat Rashid
Illustrated by Alexi Natchev

Look, Vin!

Do not run!

What is it?

It is a rat, Val!

We can run.

Look, Vin!

Do not hop!

What is it?

It is a mop, Val.

We can look at it!

Look, Vin!

Do not ride!

What is it?

It is a van.

We can hop!

Look, Val!

It is my house.

We can sit!

Val and Vin

Written by Megan Balrecht
Illustrated by Don Sullivan

Scott Foresman

Phonics Skill: Consonant *Vv*

High-Frequency Words: do, not, what

Kindergarten Reader 26

Phonics Skill:
Consonant *Vv*

High-Frequency Words:
do, not, what

Scott Foresman

scottforesman.com

Val and Vin

Written by Megan Balrecht
Illustrated by Don Sullivan

It is a jaw.

Do not jog!

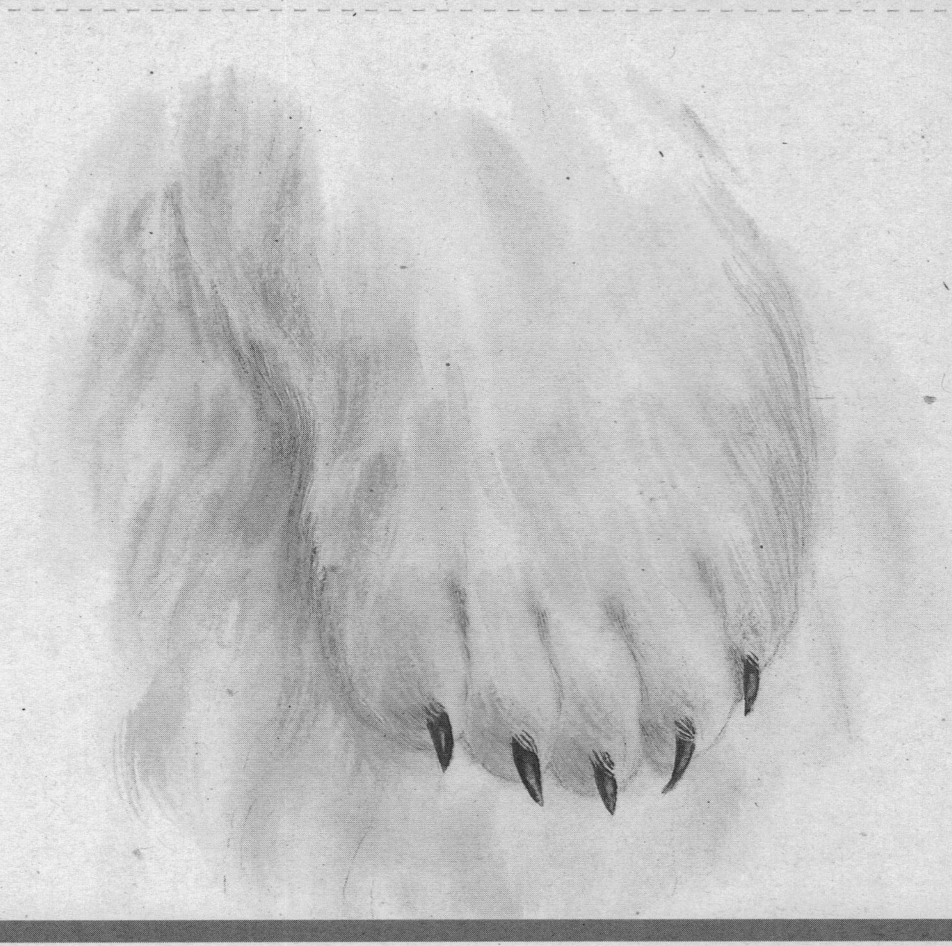

Look! What is it?

Jim can see it.

It is a bear.

Do not pat it!

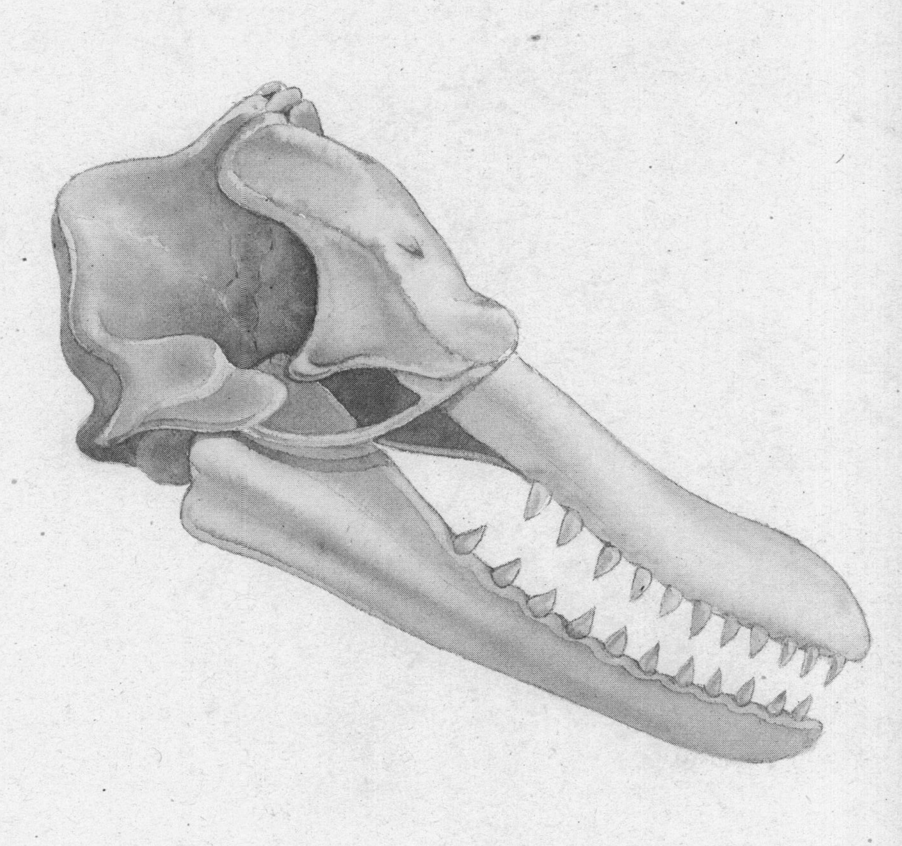

Look! What is it?

Jan can see it.

We like the museum.

We see a lot.

Look! What is it?

Jill can see it.

Do not sit on top!

We like the museum.

Written by Marge Dalton
Illustrated by Joy Dunn Keenan

Scott Foresman

Phonics Skill: Consonant *Jj*

High-Frequency Words: do, not, what

Scott Foresman Reading

Kindergarten Reader 25

Phonics Skill:
Consonant *Jj*

High-Frequency Words:
do, not, what

Scott Foresman

scottforesman.com

The Museum

Written by Marge Dalton
Illustrated by Joy Dunn Keenan

Wig has a little hat.

The hat is on a mat.

The hat has a little house.

The house is in the hat.

The house has a little rat.

The rat is in the house.

I have a little cat.

The cat is Wig.

I am little Will.

The King is big.

The rat has a watch.

The watch is big.

I have a big watch.

I am not big.

The king is big!

The Big King

Written by Lindsey Marine
Illustrated by Judy Moffatt

Scott Foresman

Phonics Skill: Consonant *Ww*

High-Frequency Words: little, have

Kindergarten Reader 24

Phonics Skill:
Consonant *Ww*

High-Frequency Words:
little, have

scottforesman.com

The Big King

Written by Lindsey Marine
Illustrated by Judy Moffatt

I have a big kangaroo.

Kim can not have it.

It is my big kangaroo.

I hid it.

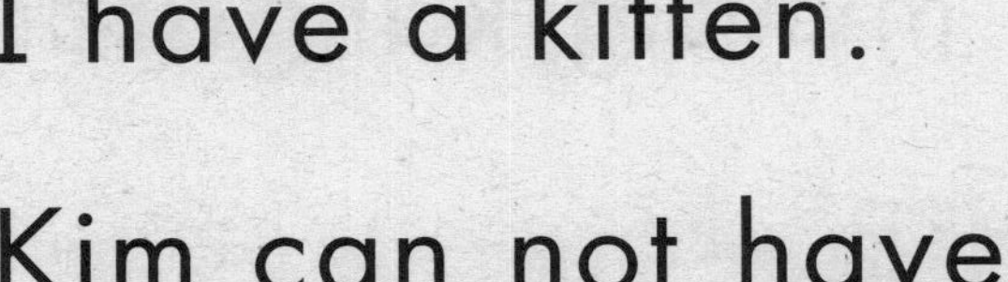

I have a kitten.

Kim can not have it.

It is my kite.

I hid it.

Kim is a little kid.

Kim got my kite.

It is my kitten.

MOM!

Kim can have the kitten.

Little Kim

Written by Katie Gillam
Illustrated by Marsha Wilborn

Scott Foresman

This book belongs to

____

Phonics Skill: Consonant *Kk*

High-Frequency Words: little, have

Scott Foresman Reading

Kindergarten Reader 23

Phonics Skill:
Consonant *Kk*

High-Frequency Words:
little, have

Scott Foresman

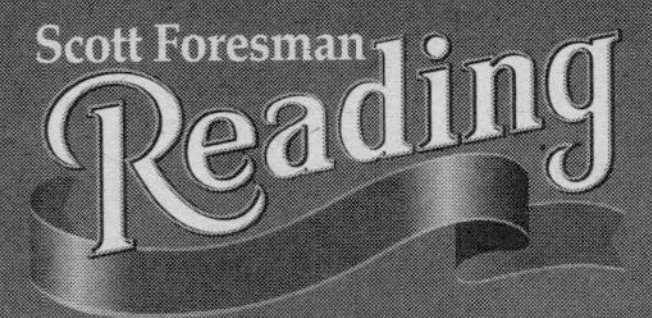

scottforesman.com

Little Kim

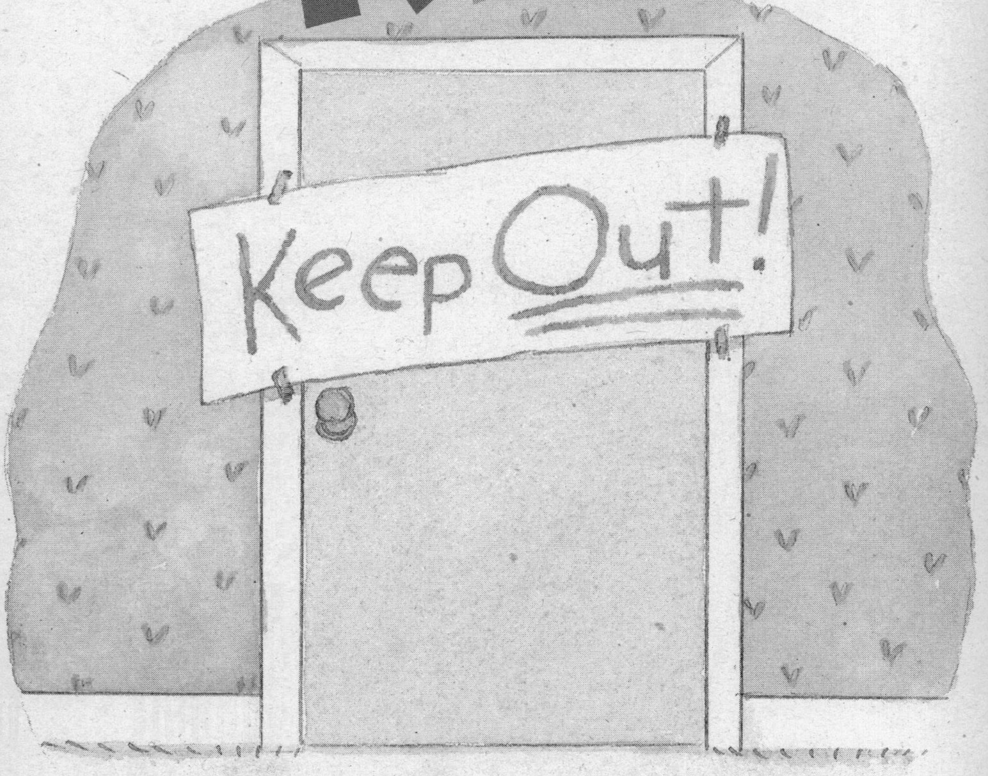

Written by Katie Gillam
Illustrated by Marsha Wilborn

We see a log house.

We see a log house in the grass.

We can hop in the log house.

We hop in it.

My, my! We see Pat the rat.

Look! We see a rat!

We can hop.

We can hop in the grass.

I am Dot.

I am Sam.

I am Tig.

We can sit on top!

Sam can hop on Tig!

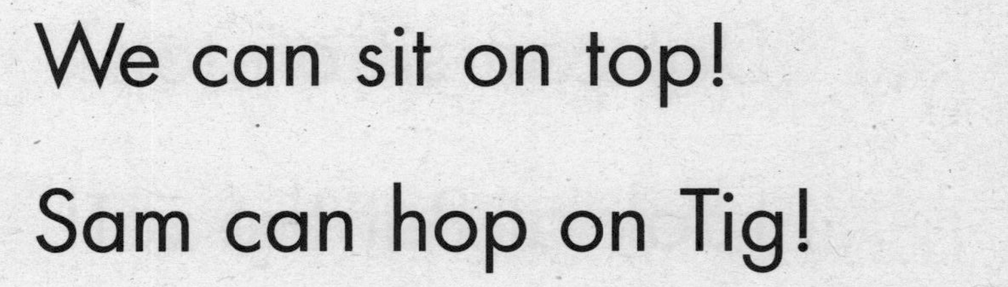

Dot can sit on top!

Look at Pat the rat!

Dot, Sam, and Tig

Written by Alexandra Rose
Illustrated by Deborah Melmon

Scott Foresman

Phonics Skill: Short Vowel *o*
High-Frequency Words: my, we

Scott Foresman **Reading**

Kindergarten Reader 22

Phonics Skill:
Short Vowel *o*

High-Frequency Words:
my, we

scottforesman.com

Dot, Sam, and Tig

Written by Alexandra Rose
Illustrated by Deborah Melmon

Tig can see my bell.

Tig can hear my bell.

Mig the pig can see my bell.

Mig the pig can hear my bell.

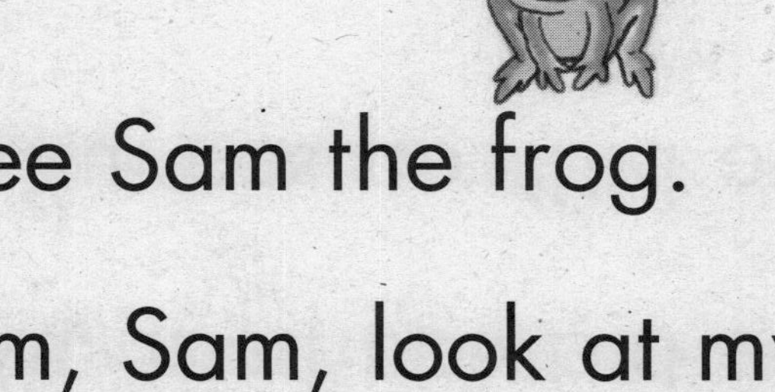

I see Sam the frog.

Sam, Sam, look at my bell.

I see Tig the dog.

Tig, Tig, look at my bell.

I am Gil.

I like my bell.

We can see the bell.

We can hear the bell.

We like the bell.

Gil's Bell

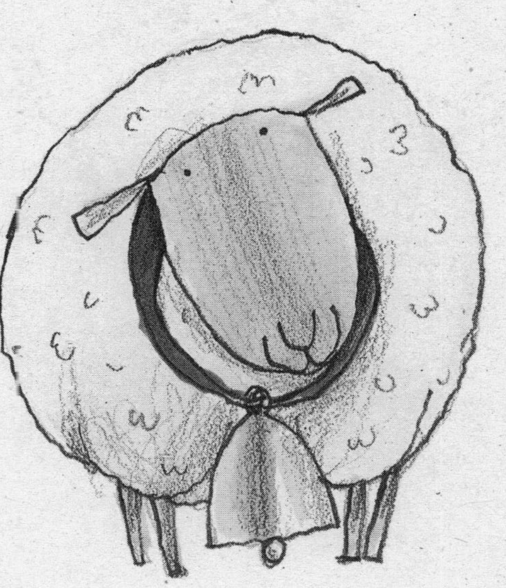

Written by Sophie Larson
Illustrated by G. Brian Karas

Scott Foresman

Phonics Skill: Consonant *Gg*

High-Frequency Words: my, we

Scott Foresman Reading

Kindergarten Reader 21

Phonics Skill:
Consonant *Gg*

High-Frequency Words:
my, we

scottforesman.com

Gil's Bell

Written by Sophie Larson
Illustrated by G. Brian Karas

Dan did it!

I pat Dan.

Look! See the book, Dan?

Dan can.

Dan did it!

I pat Dan.

Look! See the shoes, Dan?

Dan can.

Dan is a big dog.

I pat Dan.

Look! See the gum, Dan?

Dan did!

Look at Dan!

Written by Tim Surico
Illustrated by Anne Kennedy

Scott Foresman

This book belongs to

____

Phonics Skill: Consonant *Dd*

High-Frequency Words: look, see

Kindergarten Reader 20

Phonics Skill:
Consonant *Dd*

High-Frequency Words:
look, see

scottforesman.com

Written by Tim Surico
Illustrated by Anne Kennedy

Look and see.

Look and see the crab.

Look and see.

Look and see the fox.

Look and see.

Look and see the camel.

Look and see.

Look and see the frog.

Look and see.

Look and see the cat.

Look and see.

Look and see the fish.

Look and see.

Look and see the boy.

Look and See

Written by Saralya Ash

Scott Foresman

Phonics Skill: Consonant *Ll*
High-Frequency Words: look, see

Kindergarten Reader 19

Phonics Skill:
Consonant *Ll*

High-Frequency Words:
look, see

Scott Foresman

scottforesman.com

Look and See

Written by Saralya Ash

I like it, Tim the horse.

I like it, Pat the rat.

I like it, Ann the hen.

I like it, Nan the cat.

I like it, Sam the dog.

The hat is a hit!

But I like it!

I Like It!

Written by Babs Blaney
Illustrated by Ruth Flannigan

Scott Foresman

Phonics Skill: Consonant *Rr*

High-Frequency Words: but, it

Scott Foresman Reading

Kindergarten Reader 18

Phonics Skill:
Consonant *Rr*

High-Frequency Words:
but, it

scottforesman.com

I Like It!

Written by Babs Blaney
Illustrated by Ruth Flannigan

Can Nan hit it?

Nan can hit it!

Nat can sit.

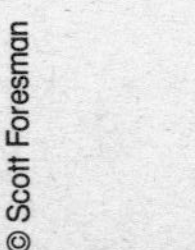

Pam can hit it!

Can Pam hit it?

But can Nat hit it?

Nat can hit it!

Written by C. Budzisz
Illustrated by Lindy Burnett

Scott Foresman

This book belongs to

____

Phonics Skill: Consonant *Hh*

High-Frequency Words: but, it

Scott Foresman Reading

Kindergarten Reader 17

Phonics Skill:
Consonant *Hh*

High-Frequency Words:
but, it

Scott Foresman

scottforesman.com

We Can Hit It!

Written by C. Budzisz
Illustrated by Lindy Burnett

The grass is green.

I am at the big tree.

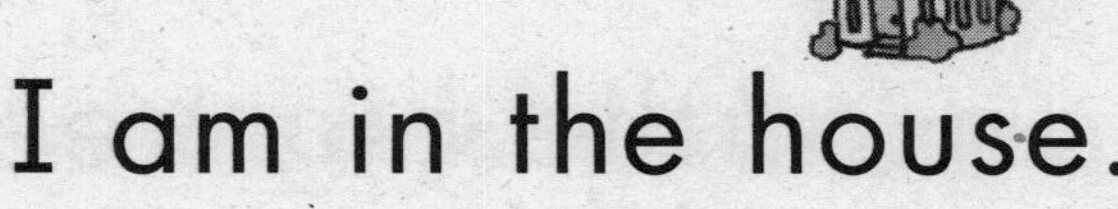

I am in the house.

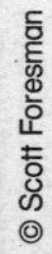

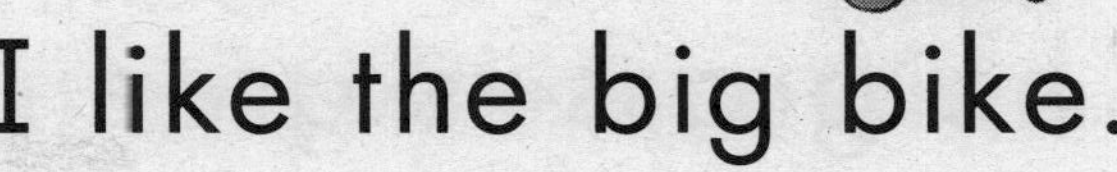

I like the big bike.

I am a pink pig.

The mat is pink.

I am a purple pig!

Pink Pig

Written by Susan Hayes
Illustrated by Sheila Lucas

Scott Foresman

Phonics Skill: Short Vowel *i*

High-Frequency Words: big, in

Scott Foresman Reading

Kindergarten Reader 16

Phonics Skill:
Short Vowel *i*

High-Frequency Words:
big, in

scottforesman.com

Pink Pig

Written by Susan Hayes
Illustrated by Sheila Lucas

Is the fish in?

The fish is in.

Can the bird nap?

The pig is big.

Is the pig big?

The bird can nap.

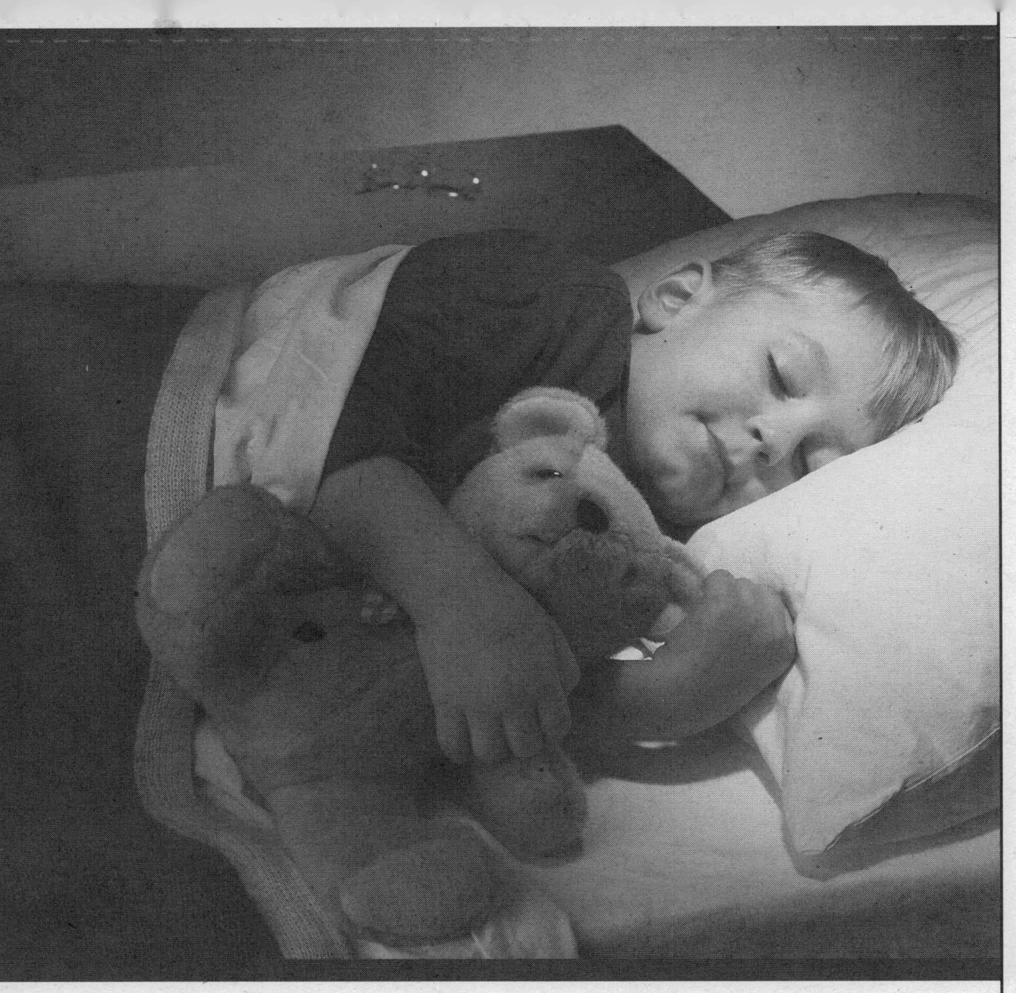

Like Nat.

Can Nat Nap?

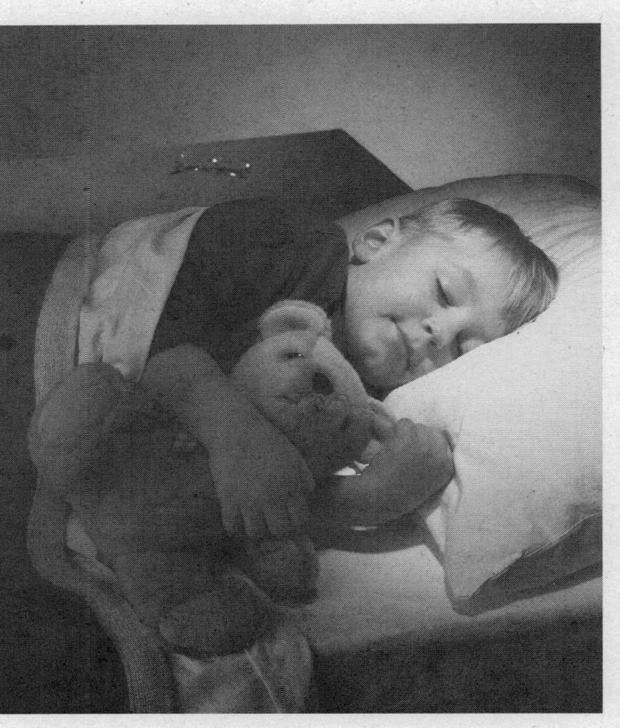

Written by Carol Hindin

Scott Foresman

Phonics Skill: Consonant *Nn*

High-Frequency Words: big, in

Photography Credits
Front Cover: Bruce Coleman, Inc./Hans Reinhard: Title page, 2. Grant Heilman Photography/John Colwell: 3. Imagery/©S.Nielsen: 7. SBG: 4, 5, 8. Tom Stack & Associates/Rod Planck: 6.

Scott Foresman Reading

Kindergarten Reader 15

Phonics Skill:
Consonant *Nn*

High-Frequency Words:
big, in

scottforesman.com

Can Nat Nap?

Written by Carol Hindin

A stick?

The stick is a rake.

A pan?

The sock is a puppet.

A sock?

Cake!

I like cake!

What Is It?

Written by Bunny Faldudo
Photographs by Michael Gaffney

Scott Foresman

This book belongs to

____

Phonics Skill: Consonant *Pp*

High-Frequency Words: like, is

Kindergarten Reader 14

Phonics Skill:
Consonant *Pp*

High-Frequency Words:
like, is

Scott Foresman

scottforesman.com

What Is It?

Written by Bunny Faldudo
Photographs by Michael Gaffney

I like Cam.

I like Mac the cat.

I like the car.

It is red.

I like the bus.

The bus is yellow.

I am Sam.

I am Cam.

The cat is Mac.

I like the plane.

The plane is gray.

I like Cam.

I like Mac the brown cat.

I like cookies.

I Like Cam!

Written by C. McCarthy
Illustrated by John Magine

Scott Foresman

Phonics Skill: Consonant *Cc*

High-Frequency Words: like, is

Scott Foresman Reading

Kindergarten Reader 13

Phonics Skill:
Consonant Cc

High-Frequency Words:
like, is

Scott Foresman

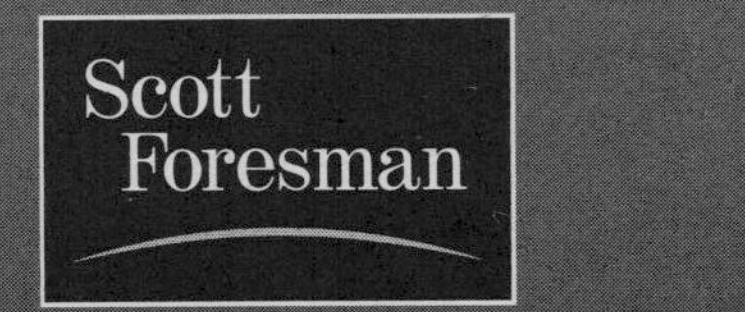

scottforesman.com

I Like Cam!

Written by C. McCarthy
Illustrated by John Magine

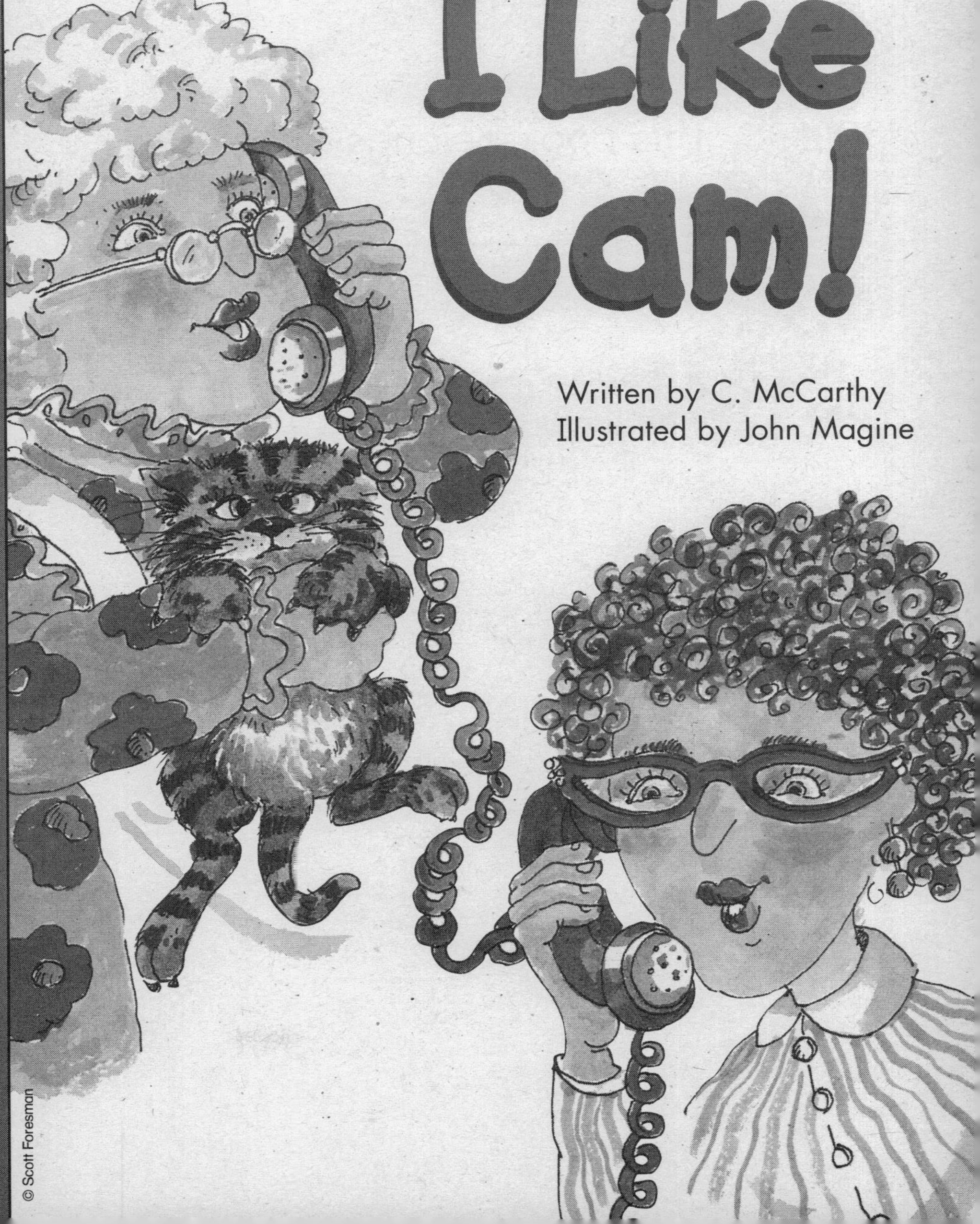

I can bat.

Bat, bat, bat!

I sat.

I am at bat.

I am Sam.

I sat at bat.

I am Sam!

Sam!

Written by Claire Talbrecht
Illustrated by Laura Ovresat

Scott Foresman

Phonics Skill: Short Vowel *a*
High-Frequency Words: I, am

Kindergarten Reader 12

Phonics Skill:
Short Vowel *a*

High-Frequency Words:
I, am

scottforesman.com

Sam!

Written by
Claire Talbrecht
Illustrated by
Laura Ovresat

Can bird?

Can cat?

Can frog?

Can dog?

Can fish?

Can fox?

I can!

I am!

Lunch Time!

Written by Patricia Rose
Illustrated by Loretta Krupiski

Scott Foresman

This book belongs to

____

Phonics Skill: Consonant *Ff*

High-Frequency Words: I, am

Scott Foresman Reading

Kindergarten Reader 11

Phonics Skill:
Consonant *Ff*

High-Frequency Words:
I, am

scottforesman.com

Lunch Time!

Written by Patricia Rose
Illustrated by Loretta Krupiski

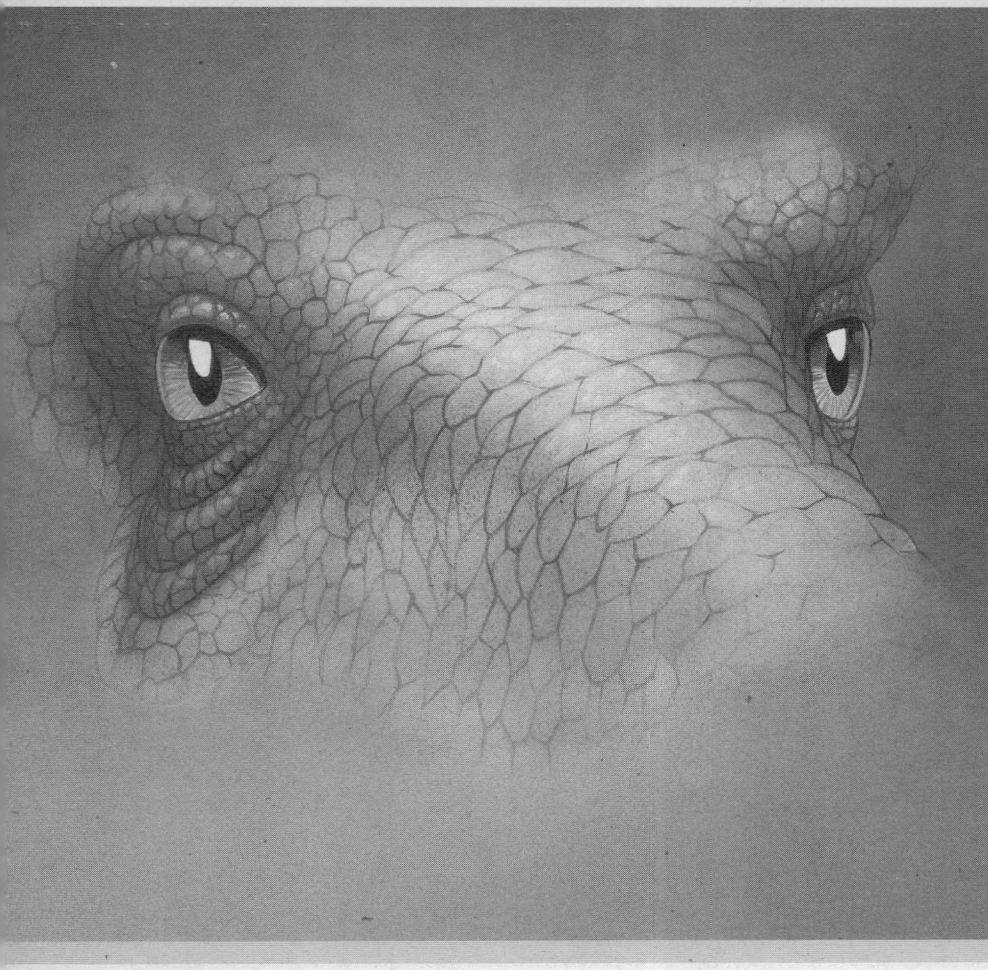

Can eyes?

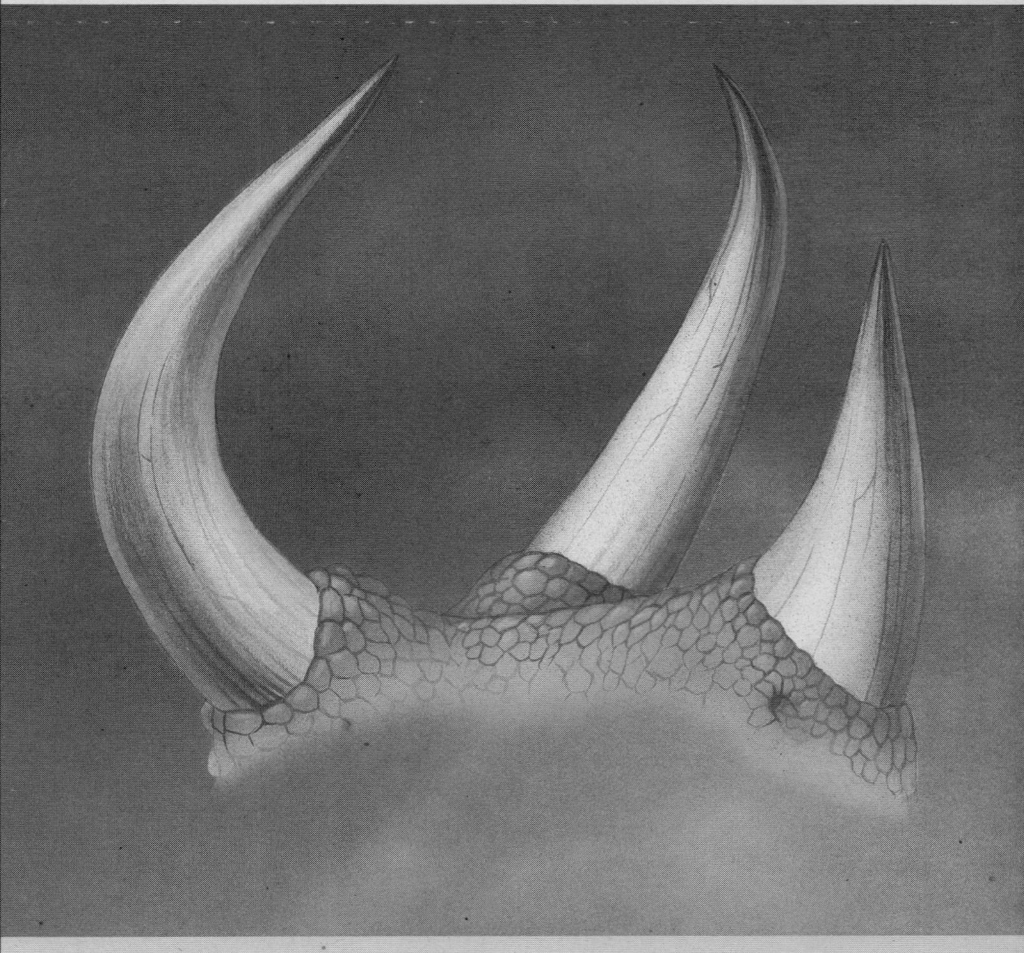

Can horns?

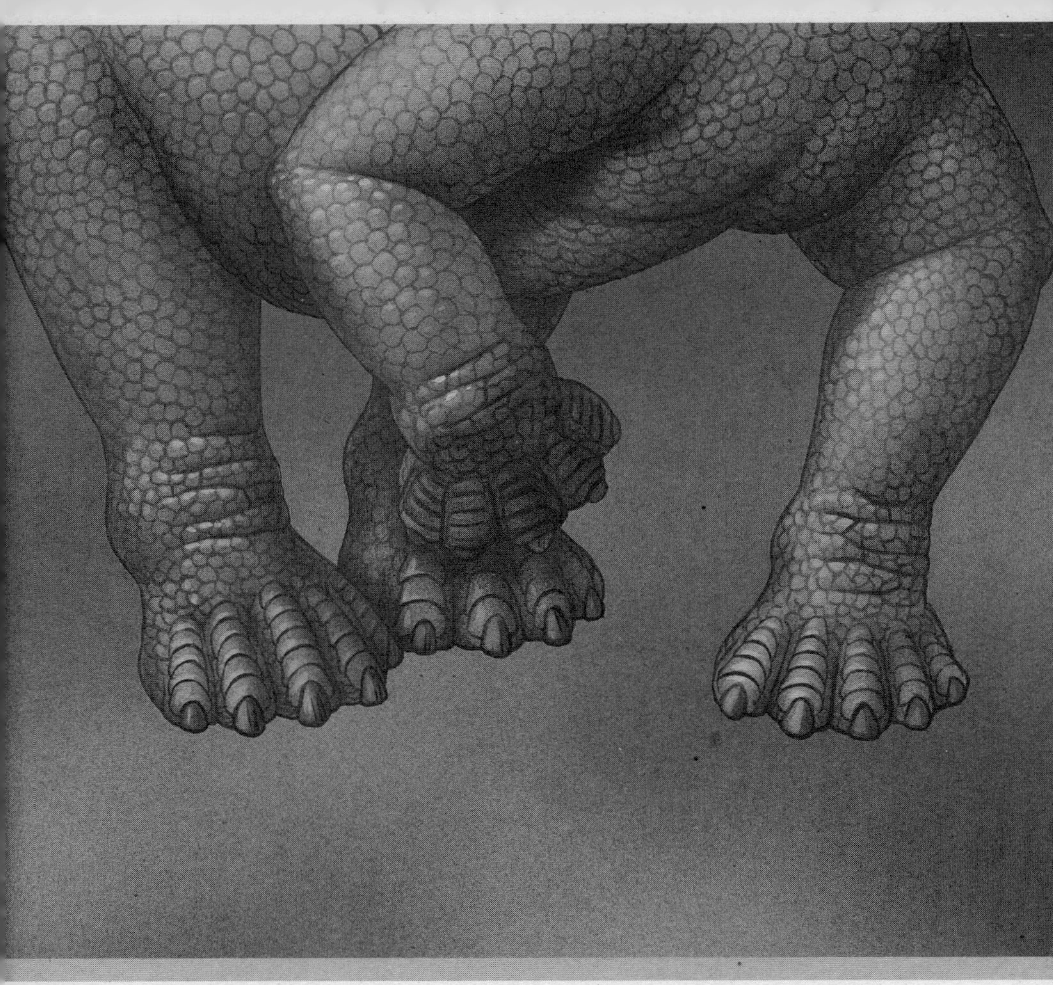

Can legs?

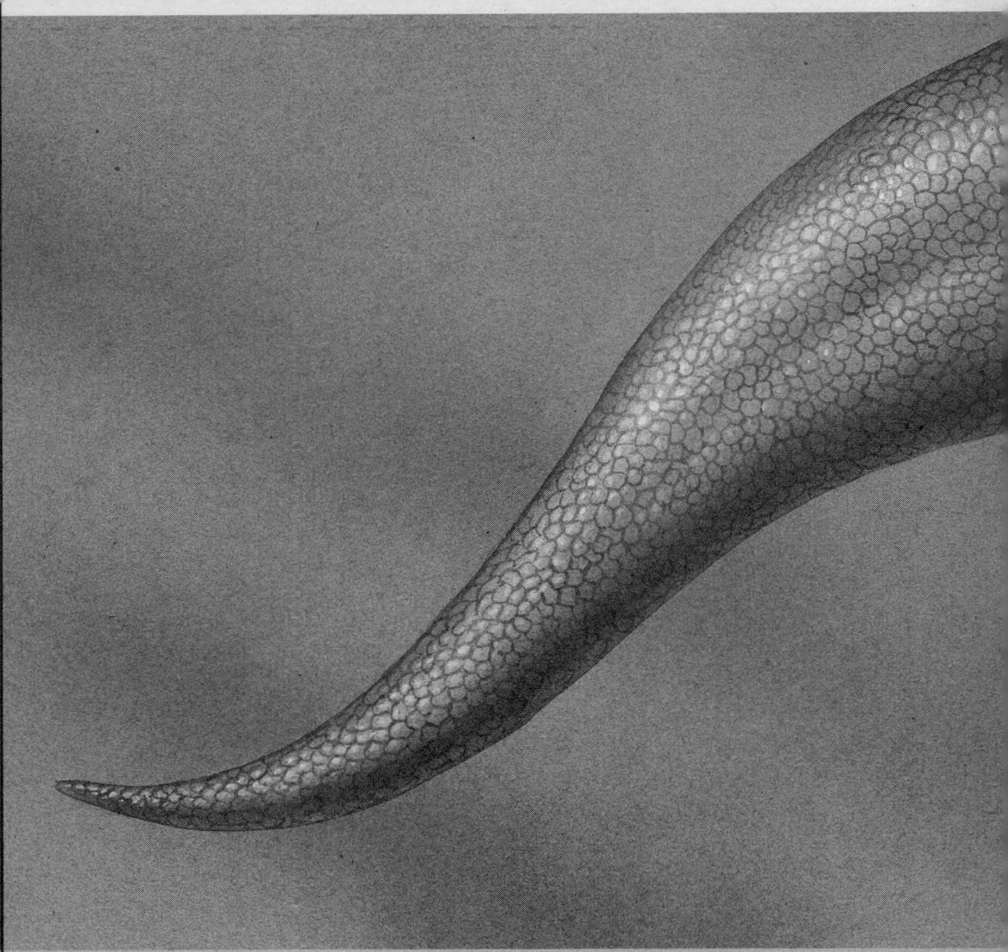

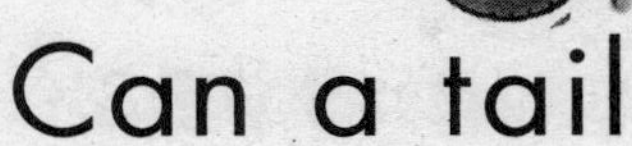

Can a tail?

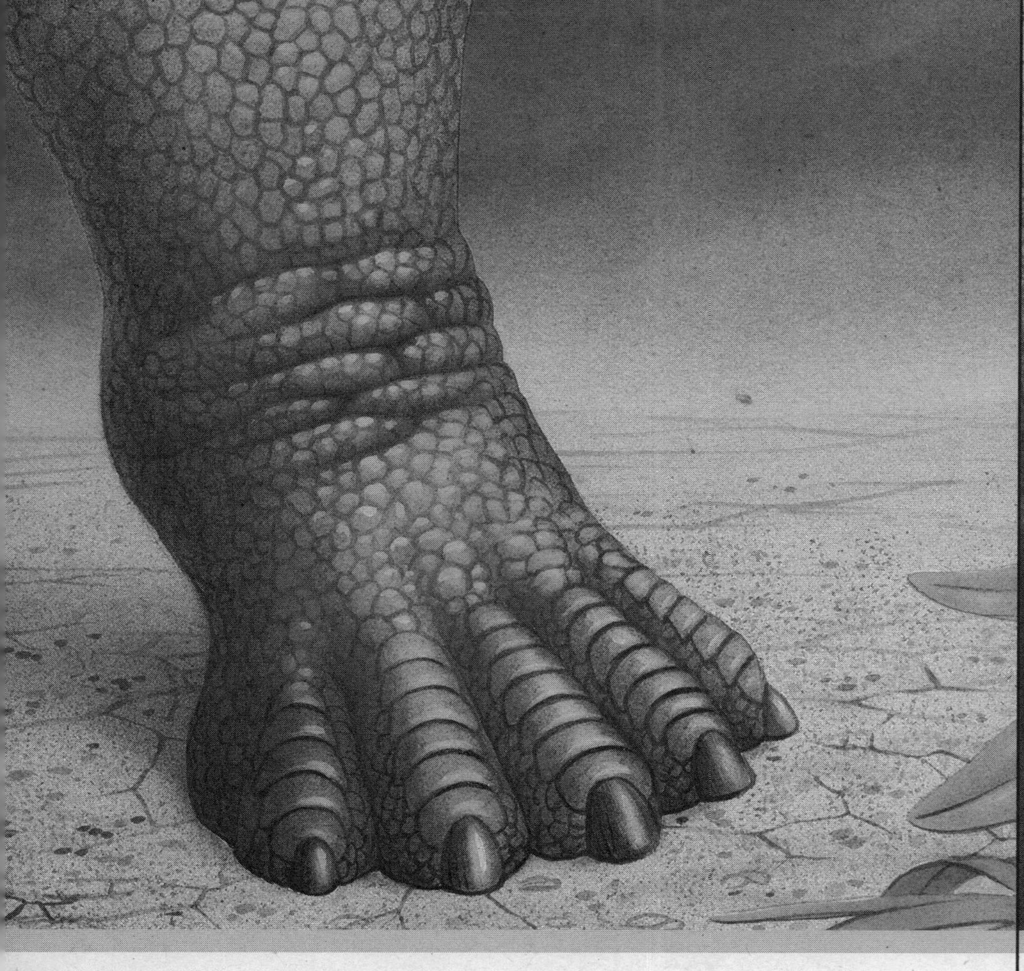

Can toes?

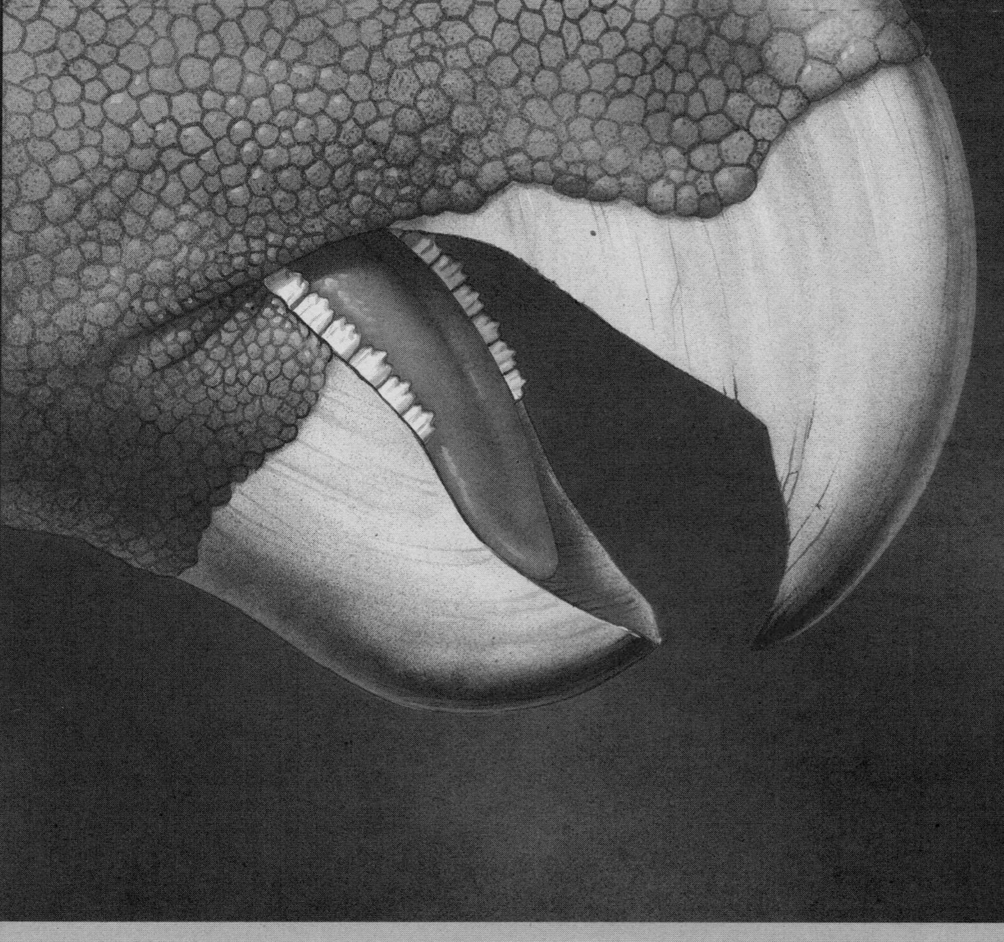

Can teeth?

At the water,
Triceratops can!

Triceratops

Written by Brian Patricks
Illustrated by Walter Stuart

Scott Foresman

Phonics Skill: Consonant *Tt*

High-Frequency Words: can, at

Scott Foresman Reading

Kindergarten Reader 10

Phonics Skill:
Consonant *Tt*

High-Frequency Words:
can, at

scottforesman.com

Triceratops

Written by Brian Patricks
Illustrated by Walter Stuart

the milk

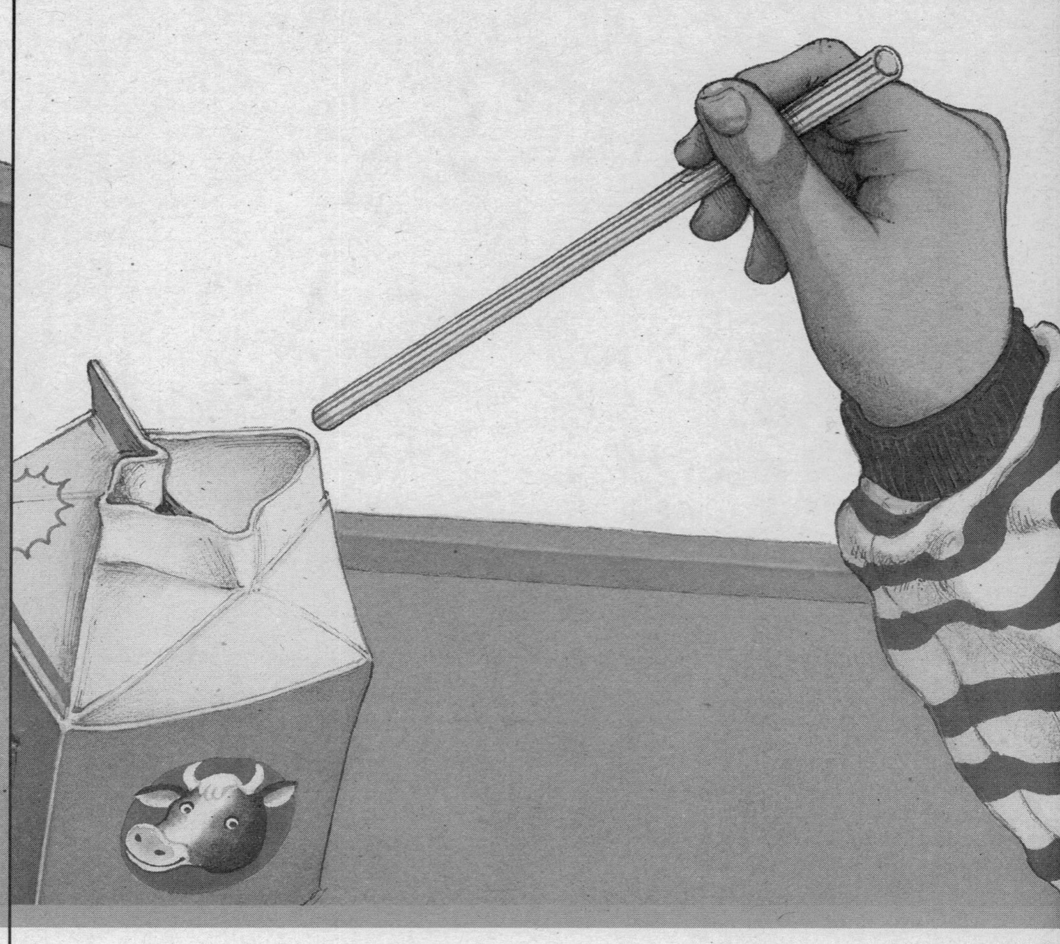

a straw

a sandwich

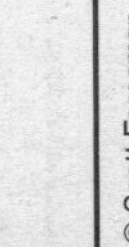

a spoon

At school, the soup

the money

The children can eat!

At School

Written by Mary Ann Doyle
Illustrated by Renée Mansfield

Scott Foresman

Phonics Skill: Consonant *Ss*

High-Frequency Words: can, at

Scott Foresman Reading

Kindergarten Reader 9

Phonics Skill:
Consonant *Ss*

High-Frequency Words:
can, at

scottforesman.com

At School

Written by Mary Ann Doyle
Illustrated by Renée Mansfield

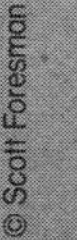

the bike

a bear

the books

a rug

the bed

a bunny

The boy!

The Boy

Written by Ryan Maher
Illustrated by Joan Holub

Scott Foresman

This book belongs to

____

Phonics Skill: Consonant *Bb*

High-Frequency Words: a, the

Scott Foresman Reading

Kindergarten Reader 8

Phonics Skill:
Consonant *Bb*

High-Frequency Words:
a, the

scottforesman.com

The Boy

Written by Ryan Maher
Illustrated by Joan Holub

the mug

the milk

a mat

a monster

a mop

Monster Mop

Written by Anthony Laurence
Illustrated by Cameron Eagle

Scott Foresman

Phonics Skill: Consonant *Mm*

High-Frequency Words: a, the

Kindergarten Reader 7

Phonics Skill:
Consonant *Mm*

High-Frequency Words:
a, the

scottforesman.com

Monster Mop

Written by Anthony Laurence
Illustrated by Cameron Eagle

cap

bear

map

book

bag

game

A nap!

The Bag

Written by Anna Albrecht
Illustrated by Priscilla Burris

Scott Foresman

Phonics Skill: Word Recognition

Scott Foresman Reading

Kindergarten Reader 6

Phonics Skill:
Word Recognition

Scott Foresman

scottforesman.com

The Bag

Written by Anna Albrecht
Illustrated by Priscilla Burris

bed

dog

pillows

book

girl

doll

Story time!

Story Time!

Written by Grace Winslow
Illustrated by Nneka Bennett

Scott Foresman

This book belongs to

____

Phonics Skill: Word Recognition

Kindergarten Reader 5

Phonics Skill:
Word Recognition

Scott Foresman

scottforesman.com

Story Time!

Written by Grace Winslow
Illustrated by Nneka Bennett

cars

dog

cook

cows

corn

bird

The cat!

The Cat

Written by E.E. Maher
Illustrated by Krista Brauckmann-Towns

Scott Foresman

Phonics Skill: Word Recognition

Kindergarten Reader 4

Phonics Skill:
Word Recognition

Scott Foresman

scottforesman.com

The Cat

Written by E.E. Maher
Illustrated by Krista Brauckmann-Towns

pig

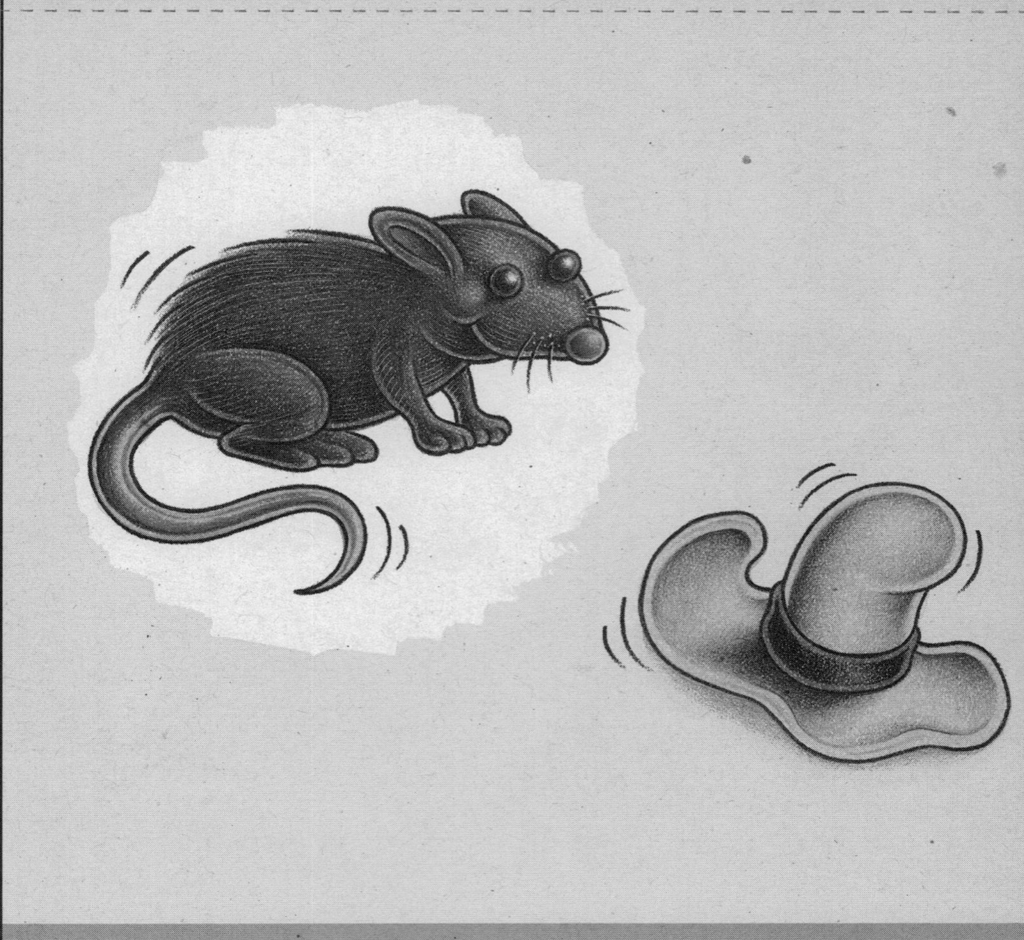

rat

dog

bat

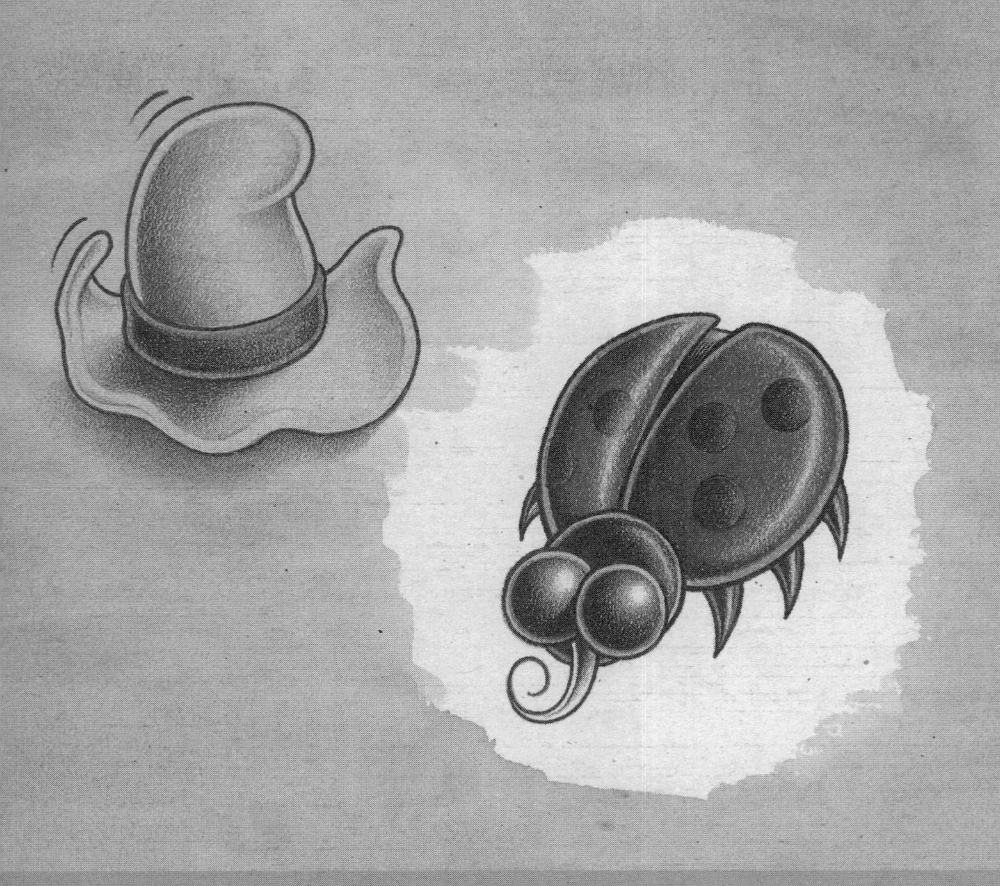

bug

cat

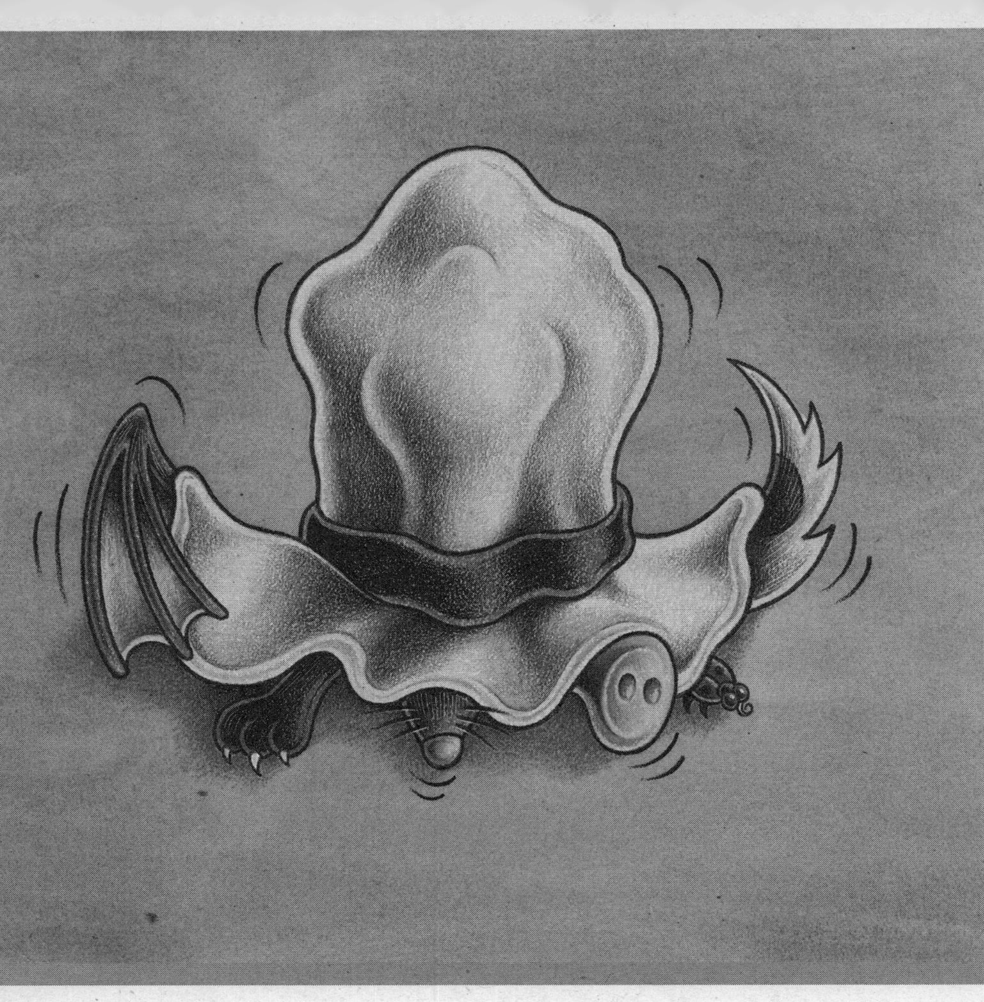

The hat!

The Hat

Written by Emily Miller
Illustrated by Gregg Valley

Scott Foresman

Phonics Skill: Word Recognition

Scott Foresman Reading

Kindergarten Reader 3

Phonics Skill:
Word Recognition

scottforesman.com

The Hat

Written by Emily Miller
Illustrated by Gregg Valley

pole

dog

boat

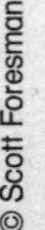

net

pail

plane

Go fish!

Go Fish!

Written by L.R. Kelly
Illustrated by Shelley Dieterichs

Scott Foresman

This book belongs to

____

Phonics Skill: Word Recognition

Scott Foresman Reading

Kindergarten Reader 2

Phonics Skill:
Word Recognition

scottforesman.com

Go Fish!

Written by L.R. Kelly
Illustrated by
Shelley Dieterichs

bike

wood

wagon

mat

window

dog

All wet!

All Wet!

Written by Wanda Marie Kamza
Illustrated by Toby Williams

Scott Foresman

Phonics Skill: Word Recognition

Scott Foresman Reading

Kindergarten Reader 1

Phonics Skill:
Word Recognition

Scott Foresman

scottforesman.com

All Wet!

Written by Wanda Marie Kamza
Illustrated by Toby Williams

Kindergarten Readers for Unit 4

Book 19 Look and See
Initial consonant *l*

Book 20 Look at Dan!
Initial consonant *d*

Book 21 Gil's Bell
Initial and final consonant *g*

Book 22 Dot, Sam, and Tig
Vowel *o*

Book 23 Little Kim
Initial consonant *k*

Book 24 The Big King
Initial consonant *w*

Kindergarten Readers for Unit 5

Book 25 The Museum
Initial consonant *j*

Book 26 Val and Vin
Initial consonant *v*

Book 27 One, Two, Three
qu

Book 28 Sick In Bed?
Vowel *e*

Book 29 A Big, Blue Box
Initial and final consonant *x*

Book 30 Yes! We Get Wet!
Initial consonant *y*

Kindergarten Readers for Unit 6

Book 31 Zebra and the Yellow Van
Initial and final consonant *z*

Book 32 In the Mud!
Vowel *u*

Book 33 The Man, the Pan, and the Egg
Phonics Review: Consonants

Book 34 Jen the Hen
Initial consonant blends

Book 35 Look!
Phonics Review: Vowels

Book 36 Bud's Bug Hut
Phonics Review: Consonants and Vowels

Table of Contents

Kindergarten Readers for Unit 1

Kindergarten Readers for Unit 2

Kindergarten Readers for Unit 3

ISBN 0-328-02300-0

11 12 13 14 15 16 17 18 DBH 08 07 06 05

Kindergarten Take-Home Readers

Editorial Offices: Glenview, Illinois • Parsippany, New Jersey • New York, New York
Sales Offices: Parsippany, New Jersey • Duluth, Georgia • Glenview, Illinois
Carrollton, Texas • Ontario, California